ISLANDS OF GUINEA-BISSAU

Table of Contents

Bissagos Islands 1
Bolama 2
Bubaque 3
Carache 3
Caravela 3
Demographics of Guinea-Bissau 4
Economy of Guinea-Bissau 5
Education in Guinea-Bissau................ 8
Formosa (Guinea-Bissau) 8
Galinhas 8
Geography of Guinea-Bissau.............. 8
Guinea-Bissau 10
History of Guinea-Bissau.................. 15
Jeta (Guinea-Bissau) 16
João Viera 16
List of heads of government of Guinea-Bissau... 17
List of heads of state of Guinea-Bissau 18
Orango.. 20
Orangozinho..................................... 20
Outline of Guinea-Bissau.................. 20
Pecixe... 23
Politics of Guinea-Bissau.................. 23
Roxa 26
Unhacomo 26
Uno (Guinea-Bissau)........................ 26
Uracane 27

Preface

Each chapter in this book ends with a URL to a hyperlinked online version. Use the online version to access related pages, websites, footnotes, tables, color photos, updates, or to see the chapter's contributors. Click the edit link to suggest changes. Please type the URL exactly as it appears. If you change the URL's capitalization, for example, it may not work.

Purchase of this book entitles you to a free trial membership in the publisher's book club at www.booksllc.net. (Time limited offer.) Simply enter the barcode number from the back cover onto the membership form on our home page. The book club entitles you to select from millions of books at no additional charge, including a PDF copy of this and related books to read on the go. Simply enter the title or subject onto the search form to find them.

If you have any questions, could you please be so kind as to consult our Frequently Asked Questions page at www.booksllc.net/faqs.cfm? You are also welcome to contact us there.

Publisher: Books LLC, Wiki Series, Memphis, TN, USA, 2013.

Bissagos Islands

Location of the Bissagos Islands in the Atlantic Ocean

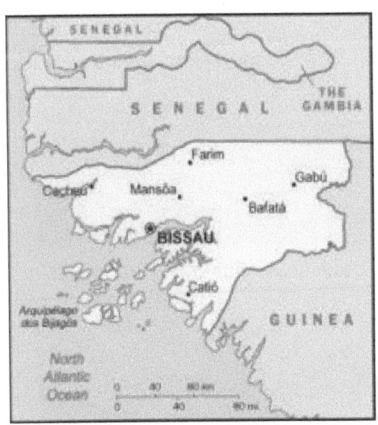

Map of Guinea Bissau with the Bissagos Islands

The **Bissagos Islands**, also spelled Bijagós Islands as in its Portuguese name (Arquipélago dos Bijagós) are a group of about 88 islands and islets located in the Atlantic Ocean and are part of the African nation of Guinea-Bissau. The archipelago was formed from the ancient delta of the Rio Geba and the Rio Grande and spans an area of 2,624 km (1,184 sq. miles).

Location coordinates: 11°40' to 14°43'N; 15°20' to 17°00'W

Only some 20 islands are populated year-round, namely Bubaque which is where the Bissagos administrative capital is situated and is the most populated island, Bolama, Carache, Caravela, Enu, Formosa, Galinhas, João Vieira, Maio, Meneque, Orango, Orangozinho, Ponta, Roxa, Rubane, Soga, Unhacomo, Uno, and Uracane.

There is a high diversity of ecosystems: mangroves with intertidal zones, palm forests, dry and semi-dry forests, secondary and degraded forests, coastal savanna, sand banks and aquatic zones. The archipelago was declared in 1996 a UNESCO Biosphere Reserve--Boloma Bijagós Biosphere Reserve, known for animals including marine turtles, hippopotamus and the southern islands are today a nature reserve.

Demographics

The population is estimated at about 30,000 (2006) and the local ethnic group known as Bidyogo (Bijagó in Portuguese predominates. It is a relatively youthful population due to high birth rates and low life expectancy even by African standards.

Economy

The economy is largely rural, with many families living from subsistence farming and fishing. There is some tourist activity, mostly boat charters from neighboring Senegal. Lack of infrastructure and communication links prevent the development of the islands' unique tourism potential.

Starting in the early 2000s, several the Bissagos islands began to be used as transit depots for narcotraffic, which is quickly changing the social and economic fabrics of the islands.

History

In pre-European colonial times, the islands were central to the trade along the coast of West Africa and they built up a powerful navy. In 1535, this enabled them to rout the Portuguese when they attempted to conquer the islands, which were not taken by Portugal until 1936.

The Bissagos were visited by Austrian anthropologist and photographer Hugo Bernatzik in 1930–1931, who documented daily life among the Bidyogo people.

Culture

Due to difficulties of communication with mainland Guinea-Bissau that persist to this day, the population has a considerable degree of autonomy and has shielded its ancestral culture from outside influence. Mostly Bidyogo (Bijago in Portuguese) is still spoken along with Portuguese and creole.

Bissagos society is charactered by age-grade progression for both men and women (separately). The grade-ascension ceremonies (generally known as "fanados") take place years apart and entail extensive preparation and ceremony. The Bissagos has a unique tradition of matriarchy, whereby it is the women who choose their husbands and terminate the matrimony; in Orango they make a single plate of food (often a traditional fish-eye platter) for the spouse-to-be, who agrees to the marriage by eating of the fish.

Art

The Bissagos peoples produce many artifacts for daily use and ritual following a traditional iconography that is unique to their culture, but shows variations from island to island. Among the most striking Bidyogo art pieces are the portable ancestor shrines ("iran") and the zoomorphic masks respresenting cows ("vaca-bruta"), sharks, stingrays and, occasionally, other local animals. Traditionally-decorated artifacts are also produced for "fanado" coming-of-age ceremonies (wood masks, spears, shields, headgear, bracelets), daily activities (fishing, agriculture) and personal use (stools, basketry, foodware). Its unique aesthetics make Bidyogo art easily distinctive from other African tribal art.

Source http://en.wikipedia.org/wiki/Bissagos_Islands

Bolama

Bolama

Italian plane crash monument with Governor's palace

Location in Guinea-Bissau
Coordinates: 11°35′N 15°28′W

Country	Guinea-Bissau
Region	Bolama Region
District	
Population (2008 (est))	
• Total	10,014

Bolama is the closest of the Bijagós Islands to the mainland of Guinea-Bissau, and is also the name of the island's main town, the capital of the Bolama Region. Population 10,014 (2008 est).

It is almost surrounded by mangrove swamps and is known for its cashew nuts. Although often visited by local people, the island was apparently uninhabited when British colonists settled it in 1792. Following a series of failures, they abandoned the island in 1794, another colonisation attempt in 1814 also being quickly ended.

The Portuguese also claimed Bolama in 1830 and a dispute developed. In 1860, the British proclaimed the island annexed to Sierra Leone, but in 1870 a commission chaired by Ulysses S. Grant awarded Bolama to Portugal. Subsequently, in 1879, Bolama became the first capital of Portuguese Guinea and remained so until its transfer to Bissau in 1941. Bissau had been founded in 1687 by Portugal as a fortified port and trading center. This transfer was needed due to the shortage of fresh water in Bolama. Bolama later became a seaplane stop, and a seaplane crash in 1931 is commemorated by a statue in the town.

The abandoned houses of the old capital provide a shelter for many thousands of enormous fruit eating bats. Every evening, these bats flock to the mainland, darkening the skies.

A fruit processing plant was built on Bolama shortly after independence of Guinea Bissau, with Dutch foreign aid. This plant produced canned juice and jelly of cashew fruit. However, it could not expand and had to shut down its operations, due to the shortage of fresh water on the island.

Attractions on the island include sandy beaches and the Bolama Governor's Palace. It is also designated as a biosphere reserve, and the Guinea-Bissauan government is aiming for it to be designated the nation's first World Heritage Site. A causeway links the island to the Ilha das Cobras.

Ubiquitous ruins at Bolama streets

Street view

Ruins of former administration building
Source http://en.wikipedia.org/wiki/Bolama

Bubaque

Bubaque

Port area of Bubaque

Location in Guinea-Bissau

Coordinates: 11°17′N 15°50′W
Country Guinea-Bissau
Region Bolama Region
District Bubaque District
Area
• **Land** 28 sq mi (70 km)
Population (2008)
• **Total** 9,244

Bubaque is one of the Bijagós Islands in Guinea-Bissau, and is also the name of its main town. Population 9,244 (2008 est).

The island is known for its wildlife and is heavily forested. It is linked by ferry to Bissau and has an airstrip. It is also where the Unesco nature reserve headquarters is situated, as well as a museum.

Transportation

The Bubaque airport serves the island.
Source http://en.wikipedia.org/wiki/Bubaque

Carache

Carache or **Caraxe** is an island in the Bissagos Islands, Guinea-Bissau. Its area is 80 km².

Navigation menu

Personal tools
Create account
Log in

Namespaces
Article
Talk

Variants

Actions

Search

Navigation
Main page
Contents
Featured content
Current events
Random article
Donate to Wikipedia

Interaction
Help
About Wikipedia
Community portal
Recent changes
Contact Wikipedia

Toolbox
What links here
Related changes
Upload file

Special pages
Permanent link
Page information
Cite this page

Print/export
Create a book
Download as PDF
Printable version

Languages
Deutsch
Español
Français
中文
Edit links
Source http://en.wikipedia.org/wiki/Carache

Caravela

Caravela is the northernmost island of the Bissagos Islands of Guinea-Bissau. The island is heavily forested with mangroves. It also has white, sandy beaches.

Data and Facts
Areal: 128 km²
Coastline: 56 km

Distance to next Island: 1 km
Distance to the Coast: 37 km
ICAO Code: GGCV

Navigation menu

Personal tools
Create account
Log in

Namespaces
Article
Talk

Variants

Actions

Search

Navigation
Main page
Contents
Featured content
Current events
Random article
Donate to Wikipedia

Interaction
Help
About Wikipedia
Community portal
Recent changes
Contact Wikipedia

Toolbox
What links here
Related changes
Upload file

Special pages
Permanent link
Page information
Cite this page

Print/export
Create a book
Download as PDF
Printable version

Languages
Deutsch
Español
Esperanto
Français
Latina
Nederlands
日本語
Português
中文
Edit links
Source   http://en.wikipedia.org/wiki/
Caravela

Demographics of Guinea-Bissau

This article is about the demographic features of the population of Guinea-Bissau, including population density, ethnicity, education level, health of the populace, economic status, religious affiliations and other aspects of the population. The population of Guinea-Bissau is ethnically diverse with distinct languages, customs, and social structures. Most Guineans, 99%, are blacks — mostly Fula and Mandinka-speakers concentrated in the north and northeast, the Balanta and Papel, living in the southern coastal regions, and the Manjaco and Mancanha, occupying the central and northern coastal areas. Most of the rest are *mestiços* of mixed Portuguese and black descent, including Cape Verdean minority. Due to the exodus of most Portuguese settlers after independence, less than 1% of Guinea-Bissauans are pure Portuguese. The country also has a Chinese minority, including Macanese people of mixed Portuguese and Chinese blood from Macau. Most people are farmers. 50% are Muslims — this makes Guinea-Bissau the only Portuguese-speaking nation with a Muslim majority and most Muslims are Sunnis; 40% are pagans, principally Fula and Mandinka. Less than 10% are Christians, mostly Roman Catholics.

Population

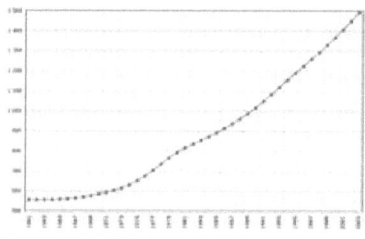

According to the 2010 revison of the World Population Prospects the total population was 1 515 000 in 2010, compared to only 518 000 in 1950. The proportion of children below the age of 15 in 2010 was 41.3%, 55.4% was between 15 and 65 years of age, while 3.3% was 65 years or older.

	Total population (x 1000)	Population aged 0–14 (%)	Populatio aged 15–64 (%)
1950	518	38.8	57.6
1955	566	41.9	54.9
1960	593	41.3	55.7
1965	598	41.3	55.6
1970	603	37.0	59.7
1975	694	41.0	55.7
1980	835	42.1	54.4
1985	922	45.4	51.1
1990	1 017	43.8	52.8
1995	1 125	44.1	52.6
2000	1 241	43.1	53.6
2005	1 368	42.4	54.4
2010	1 515	41.3	55.4

Vital statistics

Registration of vital events is in Guinea-Bissau not complete. The Population Departement of the United Nations prepared the following estimates.

Period	Live births per year	Deaths per year	Natural change per year	CBR*
1950-1955	30 000	18 000	12 000	54.9
1955-1960	25 000	17 000	7 000	42.3

1960-1965	25 000	16 000	9 000	42.3
1965-1970	21 000	15 000	6 000	35.6
1970-1975	36 000	18 000	18 000	55.7
1975-1980	35 000	19 000	15 000	45.5
1980-1985	42 000	21 000	21 000	47.9
1985-1990	44 000	21 000	23 000	45.8
1990-1995	48 000	23 000	26 000	45.2
1995-2000	51 000	24 000	27 000	42.8
2000-2005	54 000	24 000	29 000	41.1
2005-2010	57 000	25 000	32 000	39.3

* CBR = crude birth rate (per 1000); CI (per 1000); NC = natural change (per 1(mortality rate per 1000 births; TFR = tc

CIA World Factbook demographic statistics

The following demographic statistics are from the CIA World Factbook, unless otherwise indicated.

Population: 1,596,677 (July 2011 est.)

Population growth rate: 1.988% (2011 est.)

Sex ratio:
at birth: 1.03 male(s)/female
under 15 years: 1 male(s)/female
15-64 years: 0.9 male(s)/female
65 years and over: 0.83 male(s)/female
total population: 0.94 male(s)/female (2000 est.)

Life expectancy at birth:
total population: 49.04 years
male: 46.77 years
female: 51.37 years (2000 est.)

of children per woman)

Nationality:
noun: Guinean (s)
adjective: Guinean

Ethnic groups: African 99% (Balanta 30%, Fula 20%, Manjaca 14%, Mandinga 13%, Papel 7%), European (entirely Portuguese) and Mulatto less than 1%

Religions: Muslim 50%, indigenous beliefs 40%, Christian 10% (see Religion in Guinea-Bissau)

Languages: Portuguese (official), Crioulo, African languages

Literacy:
definition: age 15 and over can read and write
total population: 42.4%
male: 58.1%
female: 27.4% (2003 est.)

Source http://en.wikipedia.org/wiki/Demographics_of_Guinea-Bissau

Economy of Guinea-Bissau

Economy of Guinea-Bissau	
Currency	CFA franc
Fiscal year	Calendar Year
Trade organisations	AU, WTO
Statistics	
GDP	$1.938 billion (2011)
	Rank: 189st (2011)
GDP growth	4.8% (2011)
GDP per capita	$1,100 (2011)
GDP by sector	agriculture (55.7%), industry (12.7%), services (31.6%) (2011)
Inflation (CPI)	5.2% (2011)
Population below poverty line	N/A (2011)
Labour force	632,700 (2007)
Labour force by occupation	agriculture (82%)(2000)industry and services (18%)(2000)
Unemployment	N/A (2011)
Main industries	agricultural products processing, beer, soft drinks
Ease of Doing Business Rank	176thst
External	
Exports	$142.3 million (2011)
Export goods	cashew nuts, shrimp, peanuts, palm kernels, sawn lumber, rice, corn, beans, cotton, cassava, fish
Main export partners	India 76.9%, Nigeria 16.6% (2010)
Imports	$239.5 million (2011)
Import goods	foodstuffs, machinery and transport equipment, petroleum products
Main import partners	Senegal 21.8%, Portugal 20.5%, Brazil 5.6%, Cuba 4.1% (2010)
Public finances	
Public debt	N/A (2011)
Revenues	$176.2 million (2011)
Expenses	$196.5 million (2011)
Economic aid	N/A (recipient)(2011)
Credit rating	$115.9 million (2011)
Foreign reserves	$168.6 million (2009)

Main data source: CIA World Fact Book

All values, unless otherwise stated, are in US dollars

Guinea-Bissau is among the world's least developed nations and one of the 10 poorest countries in the world, and depends mainly on agriculture and fishing. Cashew crops have increased remarkably in recent years, and the country now ranks sixth in cashew production. Guinea-Bissau exports fish and seafood along with small amounts of peanuts, palm kernels, and timber. License fees for fishing provide the government with some revenue. Rice is the major crop and staple food.

History

Early colonialism

The flag of the Guinea Company, a Portuguese company that traded in several commodities and slaves around the Guinea coast from the 15th century.

From the viewpoint of European history the Guinea Coast is associated mainly with slavery. Indeed one of the alternative names for the region was the Slave Coast. When the Portuguese first sailed down the Atlantic coast of Africa in the 1430s, they were interested in gold. Ever since Mansa Musa, king of the Mali Empire, made his pilgrimage to Mecca in 1325, with 500 slaves and 100 camels (each carrying gold) the region had become synonymous with such wealth. The trade from sub-Saharan Africa was controlled by the Islamic Empire which stretched along Africa's northern coast. Muslim trade routes across the Sahara, which had existed for centuries, involved salt, kola, textiles, fish, grain and slaves. As the Portuguese extended their influence around the coast, Mauritania, Senegambia (by 1445) and Guinea, they created trading posts. Rather than becoming direct competitors to the Muslim merchants, the expanding market opportunities in Europe and the Mediterranean resulted in increased trade across the Sahara. In addition, the Portuguese merchants gained access to the interior via the Sénégal and Gambia rivers which bisected long-standing trans-Saharan routes. The Portuguese brought in copper ware, cloth, tools, wine and horses. Trade goods soon also included arms and ammunition. In exchange, the Portuguese received gold (transported from mines of the Akan deposits), pepper (a trade which lasted until Vasco da Gama reached India in 1498) and ivory. There was a very small market for African slaves as domestic workers in Europe, and as workers on the sugar plantations of the Mediterranean. However, the Portuguese found they could make considerable amounts of gold transporting slaves from one trading post to another, along the Atlantic coast of Africa. Muslim merchants had a high demand for slaves, which were used as porters on the trans-Saharan routes, and for sale in the Islamic Empire. The Portuguese found Muslim merchants entrenched along the African coast as far as the Bight of Benin. Before the arrival of the Europeans, the African slave trade, centuries old in Africa, was not yet the major feature of the coastal economy of Guinea. The expansion of trade occurs after the Portuguese reach this region in 1446, bringing great wealth to several local slave trading tribes. The Portuguese used slave labour to colonize and develop the previously uninhabited Cape Verde islands where they founded settlements and grew cotton and indigo. They then traded these goods, in the estuary of the Geba River, for black slaves captured by other black peoples in local African wars and raids. The slaves were sold in Europe and, from the 16th century, in the Americas. The Company of Guinea was a Portuguese governative institution whose task was to deal with the spices and to fix the prices of the goods. It was called *Casa da Guiné*, *Casa da Guiné e Mina* from 1482 to 1483 and *Casa da Índia e da Guiné* in 1499. The local African rulers in Guinea, who prosper greatly from the slave trade, have no interest in allowing the Europeans any further inland than the fortified coastal settlements where the trading takes place. The Portuguese presence in Guinea was therefore largely limited to the port of Bissau.

Colonial era

As with the other Portuguese territories in mainland Africa (Portuguese Angola and Portuguese Mozambique), Portugal exercised control over the coastal areas of Portuguese Guinea when first laying claim to the whole region as a colony. For three decades there are costly and continuous campaigns to suppress the local African rulers. However, by 1915 this process was complete, enabling Portuguese colonial rule to progress in a relatively unruffled state - until the emergence of nationalist movements all over Africa in the 1950s. For a brief period in the 1790s the British attempted to establish a rival foothold on an offshore island, at Bolama, but by the 19th century the Portuguese were sufficiently secure in Bissau to regard the neighbouring coastline as their own special territory. It was therefore natural for Portugal to lay claim to this region, soon to be known as Portuguese Guinea, when the European scramble for Africa began in the 1880s. Britain's interest in the region declined since the end of the British slave trade in 1807. After the abolition of slavery in the Portuguese overseas territories in the 1830s, the slave trade definitely went into serious decline. Portugal's main rival was the French, their colonial neighbours along the coast on both sides - in Senegal and in the region which became French Guinea. The Portuguese presence in Guinea was not disputed by the French. The only point at issue was the precise line of the borders. This was established by agreement between the two colonial powers in two series of negotiations, in 1886 and 1902-5. Until the end of the 19th century, rubber was the main export.

As an overseas province

In 1951, when the Portuguese government overhauled the entire colonial system, all Portugal's colonies, including Portuguese Guinea, were renamed Overseas Provinces (*Províncias Ultramarinas*). New infrastructures were built for education, health, agriculture, transportation, commerce, services, and administration. Cashew, peanut, rice, timber, livestock and fish were the main economic productions. The port of Bissau was one of the main employers and a very important source of taxes for the province's authorities.

Independence war

The fight for independence began in 1956, when Amílcar Cabral founded the *Partido Africano da Independência da Guiné e Cabo Verde* (Portuguese: *African Party for the Independence of Guinea and Cape Verde*), the PAIGC. In 1961, when a purely political campaign for independence had made predictably little progress, the PAIGC adopted guerrilla tactics. Although heavily outnumbered by Portuguese troops (approximately 30,000 Portuguese to some 10,000 guerrillas), the PAIGe had the great advantage of safe havens over the border in Senegal and Guinea, both recently independent of French rule. Several communist countries supported the guerrillas with weapons and military training. The conflict in Portuguese

Guinea involving the PAIGC guerrillas and the Portuguese Army was the most intense and damaging of all Portuguese Colonial War. Thus, during the 1960s and early 1970s, Portuguese development plans promoting strong economic growth and effective socioeconomic policies, like those applied by the Portuguese in the other two theaters of war (Portuguese Angola and Portuguese Mozambique), were not possible. In 1972 Cabral sets up a government in exile in Conakry, the capital of neighbouring Guinea. It was there, in 1973, that he was assassinated outside his house - just a year before a left-wing military coup in Portugal dramatically altered the political situation. By 1973 the PAIGC controlled most of the interior of the country, while the coastal and estuary towns, including the main populational and economic centres remained under Portuguese control. The village of Madina do Boé in the southeasternmost area of the territory, close to the border with neighbouring Guinea, was the location where PAIGC guerrillas declared the independence of Guinea-Bissau on September 24, 1973. The war in the colonies was increasingly unpopular in Portugal itself as the people got weary of war and balked at its ever-rising expense. Following the coup d'état in Portugal in 1974, the new left-wing revolutionary government of Portugal began to negotiate with the PAIGC and decided to offer independence to all the overseas territories.

After independence

As his brother Amílcar Cabral had been assassinated in 1973, Luís Cabral became the first president of independent Guinea-Bissau after independence was granted on September 10, 1974. Already as the President of Guinea-Bissau, Luís Cabral tried to impose a planned economy in the country, and supported a socialist model that left the economy of Guinea-Bissau itself ruined. Similarly, the repression the authoritarian single-party regime he led imposed on the population and severe food shortages also left marks and, despite having always denied, Luís Cabral was accused of being responsible for the death of a large number of black Guinea-Bissauan soldiers who had fought along with the Portuguese Army against the PAIGC guerrillas during the Portuguese Colonial War. Luís Cabral served from 1974 to 1980, when a military coup d'état led by João Bernardo "Nino" Vieira deposed him. After the military coup, in 1980 PAIGC admitted in its official newspaper "Nó Pintcha" (dated November 29, 1980) that many were executed and buried in unmarked collective graves in the woods of Cumerá, Portogole and Mansabá. All these events did not help the new-country to reach the level of prosperity, economic growth and development the new rulers had promised to its population.

Macro-economic trend

Guinea-Bissau Export Treemap

This is a chart of trend of gross domestic product of Guinea-Bissau at market prices estimated by the International Monetary Fund and EconStats with figures in millions of CFA Francs.

Year	Gross Domestic Product
1990	70,699
1995	124,100
2000	153,400
2005	280,000

Current GDP per capita of Guinea-Bissau grew just 3.40% in the turbulent 1970s and reached a peak growth of 71% in the 1980s. But this proved unsustainable and it consequently shrank by 34% in the 1990s. Average wages in 2007 hover around $1–2 per day.

Intermittent fighting between Senegalese-backed government troops and a military junta destroyed much of the country's infrastructure and caused widespread damage to the economy in 1998; the civil war led to a 28% drop in GDP that year, with partial recovery in 1999. Agricultural production is estimated to have fallen by 17% during the conflict, and the civil war led to a 28% overall drop in GDP in 1998. Cashew nut output, the main export crop, declined in 1998 by an estimated 30%. World cashew prices dropped by more than 50% in 2000, compounding the economic devastation caused by the conflict. Real GDP has steadily grown at an average of 2.3% from 2003 onwards.

Before the war, trade reform and price liberalization were the most successful part of the country's structural adjustment program under IMF sponsorship. The tightening of monetary policy and the development of the private sector had also begun to reinvigorate the economy. Under the government's post-conflict economic and financial program, implemented with IMF and World Bank input, real GDP recovered in 1999 by almost 8%. In December 2000 Guinea-Bissau qualified for almost $800 million in debt-service relief under the first phase of the enhanced HIPC initiative and is scheduled to submit its Poverty Reduction Strategy Paper in March 2002. Guinea-Bissau will receive the bulk of its assistance under the enhanced HIPC initiative when it satisfies a number of conditions, including implementation of its Poverty Reduction Strategy Paper.

Because of high costs, the development of petroleum, phosphate, and other mineral resources is not a near-term prospect. It produces 400,000 barrels/day of petrol.

Mean wages were $0.52 per manhour in 2009.

Income from waste dumping

In the 1980s Guinea-Bissau was part of a trend in the African continent toward the dumping of waste as a source of income. Plans to import toxic waste from Europe were cancelled after an international campaign to halt the trade. The government was offered a contract to dispose of 15 million tons of toxic wastes over a 15-year period. The income from it was equivalent to twice the value of its external debt. After strong pressure from other African countries and environmental groups the Guinea-Bissau government renounced the deal.

Drug trafficking

Over the last decade European consumption of cocaine is believed to have tripled, and West Africa has become a primary transit point for trafficking the drug from Colombia to Europe. Guinea-Bissau is the leading West African country in this regard, with smugglers taking advantage of government corruption and disorder to operate unimpeded. The army and police are alleged to be complicit and turn a blind eye to drug shipments from Latin America. Planes fly in, and sometimes use Guinea-Bissau's 88 remote islands, the majority of which are uninhabited.

Source http://en.wikipedia.org/wiki/Economy_of_Guinea-Bissau

Education in Guinea-Bissau

Education in Guinea-Bissau is compulsory from the age of 7 to 13. In 1998, the gross primary enrollment rate was 53.5 percent, with higher enrollment ratio for males (67.7 percent) compared to females (40 percent). As of 2001, Guinea-Bissau was continuing to recover from the civil conflict of 1999, which displaced one-third of the population, destroyed many schools, and prevented most young children from attending school for at least half a year.

Source http://en.wikipedia.org/wiki/Education_in_Guinea-Bissau

Formosa (Guinea-Bissau)

Formosa is an island in the Bissagos Islands, Guinea-Bissau. Its area is 140 km². It is located right off the West coast of the northern half of Africa.

Source http://en.wikipedia.org/wiki/Formosa_(Guinea-Bissau)

Galinhas

Galinhas is an island in the Bijagós Archipelago of Guinea-Bissau, lying south west of Bolama. Sights on the island include the former Portuguese prison and governor's house. Some boats from Bissau to Bubaque call at the island.

Navigation menu

Personal tools

Create account
Log in

Namespaces

Article
Talk

Variants

Actions

Search

Navigation

Main page
Contents
Featured content
Current events
Random article
Donate to Wikipedia

Interaction

Help
About Wikipedia
Community portal
Recent changes
Contact Wikipedia

Toolbox

What links here

Related changes
Upload file
Special pages
Permanent link
Page information
Cite this page

Print/export

Create a book
Download as PDF
Printable version

Languages

Deutsch
Español
Português
中文
Edit links
Source http://en.wikipedia.org/wiki/Galinhas

Geography of Guinea-Bissau

This article describes the geography of Guinea-Bissau.

Climate

The climate in Guinea-Bissau is tropical. This means it is generally hot and humid. It has a monsoonal-type rainy season (June to November) with south-westerly winds and a dry season (December to May) with northeasterly harmattan winds.

Guinea-Bissau is warm all year around and there is little temperature fluctuation; it averages 26.3 °C (79.3 °F). The average rainfall for Bissau

Geography of Guinea-Bissau • 9

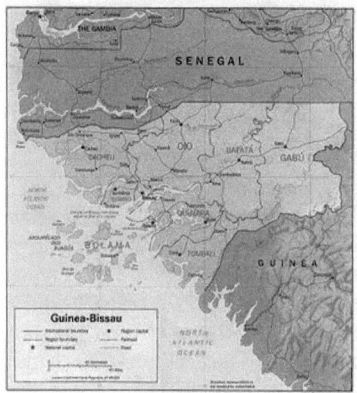
Map Of Guinea Bissau

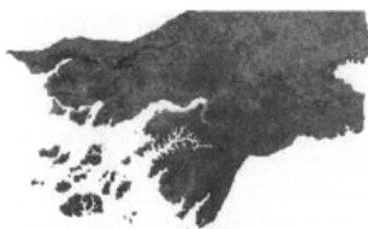
Satellite image of Guinea-Bissau

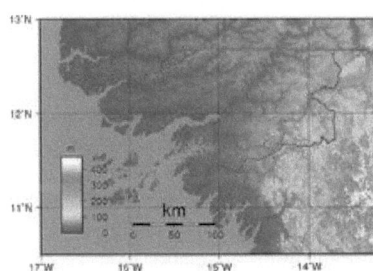
Topography of Guinea-Bissau

Typical scenery in Guinea-Bissau

is 2,024 millimetres (79.7 in) although this is almost entirely accounted for during the rainy season which falls between June and September/October. From December through April, the country experiences drought.

Terrain and ecology

The terrain of Guinea-Bissau is mostly low coastal plain with swamps of Guinean mangroves rising to Guinean forest-savanna mosaic in the east.

The lowest point on Guinea-Bissau is at sea level at the Atlantic Ocean. The highest point on Guinea-Bissau is 300 metres above sea level at an unnamed location in the northeast corner of the country.

Natural resources found in Guinea-Bissau include fish, timber, phosphates, bauxite, clay, granite, limestone and unexploited deposits of petroleum. 8.31% of the land is arable and 250 square kilometres is irrigated. Natural hazards include a hot, dry, dusty harmattan haze that may reduce visibility during the dry season and brush fires. Severe environmental issues include deforestation; soil erosion; overgrazing and overfishing.

Near the Senegal border there have been historic sightings of the Painted Hunting Dog, *Lycaon pictus*, but that endangered canid may now be extirpated in that locale.

Bissagos Islands

Information from the CIA World Factbook

Location
Western Africa, bordering the North Atlantic Ocean, between Guinea and Senegal
Geographic coordinates
12°00′N 15°00′W
Map references
Area
Total: 36,120 km²
Land: 28,000 km²
Water: 8,120 km²
Area—comparative
Slightly less than three times the size of Connecticut
Land boundaries
Total: 724 km
Border countries: Guinea 386 km, Senegal 338 km
Coastline
350 km
Maritime claims
Exclusive economic zone: 200 nmi (370.4 km; 230.2 mi)
Territorial sea: 12 nmi (22.2 km; 13.8 mi)
Terrain
Mostly low coastal plain rising to savanna in east
Elevation extremes
Lowest point: Atlantic Ocean 0 m
Highest point: Unnamed location in the northeast corner of the country 300 m
Natural resources
Fish, timber, phosphates, bauxite, unexploited deposits of petroleum
Land use
Arable land: 11%
Permanent crops: 1%
Permanent pastures: 38%
Forests and woodland: 38%
Other: 12% (1993 est.)
Irrigated land
17 km² (1993 est.)
Natural hazards
Hot, dry, dusty harmattan haze may reduce visibility during dry season; brush fires
Environment—current issues
Deforestation; soil erosion; overgrazing; overfishing
Environment—international agreements
Party to: Biodiversity, Climate Change, Desertification, Endangered Species, Law of the Sea, Wetlands
Signed, but not ratified: None of the selected agreements

Extreme points

This is a list of the extreme points of Guinea-Bissau, the points that are farther north, south, east or west than any other location.
Northernmost point – the northern section of the border with Senegal*
Easternmost point – unnamed location on the border with Guinea immediately south-west of the Guinean village of Sofan, Gabú Region
Southernmost point – unnamed headland on Ilha Cataque, Tombali Region
Westernmost point - Cap Roxo at the point where the border with Senegal en-

ters the Atlantic Ocean, Cacheu Region
*Note: Guinea-Bissau does not have a northern-most point, the border here being formed by a straight horizontal line
Source http://en.wikipedia.org/wiki/Geography_of_Guinea-Bissau

Guinea-Bissau

Republic of Guinea-Bissau
República da Guiné-Bissau (Portuguese)

Flag — Emblem

Motto:

"Unidade, Luta, Progresso" (Portuguese)

"Unity, Struggle, Progress"

Anthem:

Esta é a Nossa Pátria Bem Amada (Portuguese)

This is Our Beloved Homeland

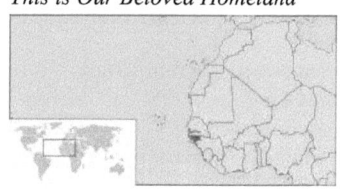

Capital and largest city	Bissau 11°52′N 15°36′W
Official languages	Portuguese
Recognised regional languages	Crioulo
Ethnic groups	30% Balanta 20% Fula 14% Manjaca 13% Mandinga 7% Papel >1% others
Demonym	Bissau-Guinean
Government	Republic
- President (acting)	Manuel Serifo Nhamadjo
- Prime Minister (acting)	Rui Duarte de Barros
Legislature	National People's Assembly
Independence from	**Portugal**
- Declared	24 September 1973
- Recognized	10 September 1974
Area	
- Total	36,125 km (136th) 13,948 sq mi
- Water (%)	22.4
Population	
- 2010 estimate	1,647,000 (148th)
- 2002 census	1,345,479
- Density	44.1/km (154th) 115.5/sq mi
GDP (PPP)	2011 estimate
- Total	$1.925 billion
- Per capita	$1,144
GDP (nominal)	2011 estimate
- Total	$969 million
- Per capita	$575
Gini (1993)	47 high
HDI (2010)	▲ 0.289 low · 164th
Currency	West African CFA franc (XOF)
Time zone	GMT (UTC+0)
Drives on the	right
Calling code	+245
ISO 3166 code	GW
Internet TLD	.gw

Guinea-Bissau, officially the **Republic of Guinea-Bissau** 🔊/ˈɡɪni bɪˈsaʊ/ (Portuguese: *República da Guiné-Bissau*, pronounced: [ʁeˈpublikɐ dɨ ɡiˈnɛ biˈsaw]), is a country in West Africa. It is bordered by Senegal to the north and Guinea to the south and east, with the Atlantic Ocean to its west. It covers 36,125 km² (nearly 14,000 sq mi) with an estimated population of 1,600,000.

Guinea-Bissau was once part of the kingdom of Gabu, as well as part of the Mali Empire. Parts of this kingdom persisted until the 18th century, while a few others were part of the Portuguese Empire since the 16th century. It then became the Portuguese colony of Portuguese Guinea in the 19th century. Upon independence, declared in 1973 and recognised in 1974, the name of its capital, Bissau, was added to the country's name to prevent confusion with the bordering Republic of Guinea. Guinea-Bissau has a history of political instability since gaining independence and no elected president has successfully served a full five-year term. On the evening of 12 April 2012, members of the country's military staged a coup and arrested the interim president and a leading presidential candidate. The military has yet to declare a current leader for the country. However, former vice chief of staff, General Mamadu Ture Kuruma has taken care of the country in the transitional period and started negotiations with opposition parties.

Only 14% of the population speaks the official language, Portuguese. A plurality of the population (44%) speaks Kriol, a Portuguese-based creole language, and the remainder speak native African languages. The main religions are African traditional religions and Islam, and there is a Christian (mostly Catholic) minority.

The country's per-capita gross domestic product is one of the lowest in the world.

Guinea-Bissau is a member of the African Union, Economic Community of West African States, Organisation of Islamic Cooperation, the Latin Union, Community of Portuguese Language Countries, La Francophonie and the South Atlantic Peace and Cooperation Zone.

History

Guinea-Bissau was once part of the kingdom of Gabu, part of the Mali Empire; parts of this kingdom persisted until the 18th century, while others were part of the Portuguese Empire. Portuguese Guinea was known also, from its main economic activity, as the Slave Coast.

Early reports of Europeans reaching this area include those of the Venetian Alvise Cadamosto's voyage of 1455, the 1479–1480 voyage by Flemish-French trader Eustache de la Fosse, and Diogo Cão who in the 1480s reached the Congo River and the lands of Bakongo, setting up thus the foundations of modern Angola, some 1200 km down the African coast from Guinea-Bissau.

Although the rivers and coast of this area were among the first places colonized by the Portuguese, since the 16th century, the interior was not explored until the 19th century. The local African rulers in Guinea, some of whom prospered greatly from the slave trade, had no interest in allowing the Europeans any further inland than the fortified coastal settlements where the trading took place. African communities that fought back against slave traders had even greater incentives to distrust European adventurers and would-be settlers. The Portuguese presence in Guinea was therefore largely limited to the port of Bissau and Cacheu, although isolated European farmer-settlers established farms along Bissau's inland rivers.

For a brief period in the 1790s, the British attempted to establish a rival foothold on an offshore island, at Bolama. But by the 19th century the Portuguese were sufficiently secure in Bissau to regard the neighbouring coastline as their own special territory, also up north in part of present South Senegal.

An armed rebellion beginning in 1956 by the African Party for the Independence of Guinea and Cape Verde (PAIGC) under the leadership of Amílcar Cabral gradually consolidated its hold on then Portuguese Guinea. Unlike guerrilla movements in other Portuguese colonies, the PAIGC rapidly extended its military control over large portions of the territory, aided by the jungle-like terrain, its easily reached borderlines with neighbouring allies and large quantities of arms from Cuba, China, the Soviet Union, and left-leaning African countries. Cuba also agreed to supply artillery experts, doctors and technicians. The PAIGC even managed to acquire a significant anti-aircraft capability in order to defend itself against aerial attack. By 1973, the PAIGC was in control of many parts of Guinea, although the movement suffered a setback in January 1973 when Cabral was assassinated.

Independence

Abandoned tank from the civil war in Bissau, 2003.

Independence was unilaterally declared on 24 September 1973. Recognition became universal following the 25 April 1974 socialist-inspired military coup in Portugal which overthrew Lisbon's Estado Novo regime.

Luís Cabral, brother of Amílcar and co-founder of PAIGC, was appointed the first President of Guinea-Bissau. Following independence local Guinean soldiers that fought along with the Portuguese Army against the PAIGC guerrillas were slaughtered by the thousands. Some managed to escape and settled in Portugal or other African nations. One of the massacres occurred in the town of Bissorã. In 1980 the PAIGC admitted in its newspaper "Nó Pintcha" (dated 29 November 1980) that many were executed and buried in unmarked collective graves in the woods of Cumerá, Portogole and Mansabá.

The country was controlled by a revolutionary council until 1984. The first multi-party elections were held in 1994, but an army uprising in 1998 led to the president's ousting and the Guinea-Bissau Civil War. Elections were held again in 2000 and Kumba Ialá was elected president.

In September 2003, a coup took place in which the military arrested Ialá on the charge of being "unable to solve the problems." After being delayed several times, legislative elections were held in March 2004. A mutiny of military factions in October 2004 resulted in the death of the head of the armed forces, and caused widespread unrest.

Vieira years

In June 2005, presidential elections were held for the first time since the coup that deposed Ialá. Ialá returned as the candidate for the PRS, claiming to be the legitimate president of the country, but the election was won by former president João Bernardo Vieira, deposed in the 1999 coup. Vieira beat Malam Bacai Sanhá in a runoff election, but Sanhá initially refused to concede, claiming that tampering occurred in two constituencies including the capital, Bissau.

Despite reports that there had been an influx of arms in the weeks leading up to the election and reports of some "disturbances during campaigning"—including attacks on government offices by unidentified gunmen—foreign election monitors labelled the election as "calm and organized". PAIGC won a strong parliamentary majority, with 67 of 100 seats, in the parliamentary election held in November 2008.

In November 2008, President Vieira's official residence was attacked by members of the armed forces, killing a guard but leaving the president unharmed. On 2 March 2009, however, Vieira was assassinated by what preliminary reports indicated to be a group of soldiers avenging the death of the head of joint chiefs of staff, General Batista Tagme Na Wai. Tagme died in an explosion on Sunday, 1 March 2009 in an assassination. Military leaders in the country have pledged to respect the constitutional order of succession. National Assembly Speaker Raimundo Pereira was appointed as an interim president until a nationwide election on 28 June 2009, which was won by Malam Bacai Sanhá.

Politics

National People's Assembly of Guinea-Bissau.

Ministry of Justice of Guinea-Bissau, Bissau

Guinea-Bissau is a republic. In the past, the government had been highly centralized, and multiparty governance has been in effect since mid-1991. The president is the head of state and the prime minister is the head of government. At the legislative level, there is a unicameral "Assembleia Nacional Popular" (National People's Assembly) made up of 100 members. They are popularly elected from multi-member constituencies to serve a four-year term. At the judicial level, there is a "Tribunal Supremo da Justiça" (Supreme Court) which consists of nine justices appointed by the president; they serve at the pleasure of the president.

Until March 2009 João Bernardo "Nino" Vieira was President of Guinea-Bissau. Elected in 2005 as an independent candidate, being declared winner of the second round by the CNE (Comité Nacional de Eleições). Vieira returned to power in 2005 after winning the presidential election only six years after being ousted from office during a civil war. Previously, he held power for 19 years after taking power in 1980 in a bloodless coup. In that action, he toppled the government of Luís Cabral. He was killed on 2 March 2009, possibly by soldiers in retaliation for the killing of the head of the joint chiefs of staff, General Batista Tagme Na Waie. This did not trigger additional violence, but there were signs of turmoil in the country, according to the advocacy group swisspeace.

In 2012, President Rachide Sambubalde Malam Bacai Sanhá died. He belonged to PAIGC (African Party for the Independence of Guinea and Cape Verde) – one of two major political parties in Guinea-Bissau along with the PRS (Party for Social Renewal) and alongside over twenty smaller parties. In the 2009 election to replace the assassinated Vieira, Sanhá was the presidential candidate of the PAIGC while Kumba Ialá was the presidential candidate of the PRS.

Regions and sectors

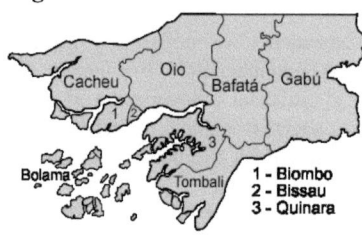

About this image

Guinea-Bissau is divided into 8 regions (*regiões*) and one autonomous sector (*sector autónomo*). These in turn are subdivided into thirty-seven sectors. The regions are:
Bafatá
Biombo
Bissau*
Bolama
Cacheu
Gabu
Oio
Quinara
Tombali

* autonomous sector

Geography

Map of Guinea Bissau

Typical scenery in Guinea-Bissau

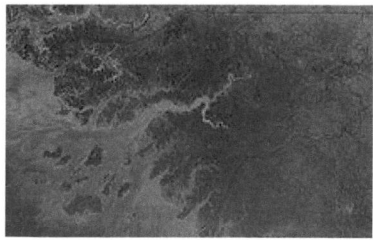

Satellite image of Guinea-Bissau (2003)

Guinea-Bissau lies mostly between latitudes 11° and 13°N (a small area is south of 11°), and longitudes 13° and 17°W.

At 36,125 square kilometres (13,948 sq mi), the country is larger in size than Taiwan, Belgium, or the U.S. state of Maryland. This small, tropical country lies at a low altitude; its highest point is 300 metres (984 ft). The interior is savanna, and the coastline is plain with swamps of Guinean mangroves. Its monsoon-like rainy season alternates with periods of hot, dry harmattan winds blowing from the Sahara. The Bijagos Archipelago extends out to sea.

Major cities

Main cities in Guinea-Bissau include:

Rank	City	Population 1979 Census	2005 estimate	Reg
1	Bissau	109,214	388,028	Biss
2	Bafatá	13,429	22,521	Bafa
3	Gabú	7,803	14,430	Gab
4	Bissorã	N/A	12,688	Oio
5	Bolama	9,100	10,769	Bola
6	Cacheu	7,600	10,490	Cac
7	Bubaque	8,400	9,941	Bola
8	Catió	5,170	9,898	Tom
9	Mansôa	5,390	7,821	Oio
10	Buba	N/A	7,779	Qui
11	Quebo	N/A	7,072	Qui
12	Canchungo	4,965	6,853	Cac
13	Farim	4,468	6,792	Oio
14	Quinhámel	N/A	3,128	Bio
15	Fulacunda	N/A	1,327	Qui

Climate

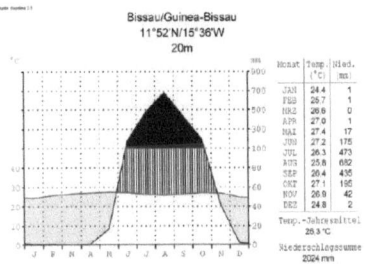

Guinea-Bissau is warm all year around and there is little temperature fluctuation; it averages 26.3 °C (79.3 °F). The average rainfall for Bissau is 2,024 millimetres (79.7 in) although this is almost entirely accounted for during the rainy season which falls between June and September/October. From December through April, the country experiences drought.

Economy

Guinea-Bissau's GDP per capita is one of the lowest in the world, and its Human Development Index is one of the lowest on earth. More than two-thirds of the population lives below the poverty line. The economy depends mainly on agriculture; fish, cashew nuts and ground nuts are its major exports. A long period of political instability has resulted in depressed economic activity, deteriorating social conditions, and increased macroeconomic imbalances. It takes longer on average to register a new business in Guinea-Bissau (233 days or about 33 weeks) than any other country in the world except Suriname. [The Economist, Pocket World in Figures, 2008 Edition, London: Profile Books]

Guinea-Bissau has started to show some economic advances after a pact of stability was signed by the main political parties of the country, leading to an IMF-backed structural reform program. The key challenges for the country in the period ahead would be to achieve fiscal discipline, rebuild public administration, improve the economic climate for private investment, and promote economic diversification. After becoming independent from Portugal in 1974 due to the Portuguese Colonial War and the Carnation Revolution, the exodus of the Portuguese civilian, military and political authorities brought tremendous damage to the country's economic infrastructure, social order and standard of living.

After several years of economic downturn and political instability, in 1997, Guinea-Bissau entered the CFA franc monetary system, bringing about some internal monetary stability. The civil war that took place in 1998 and 1999 and a military coup in September 2003 again disrupted economic activity, leaving a substantial part of the economic and social infrastructure in ruins and intensifying the already widespread poverty. Following the parliamentary elections in March 2004 and presidential elections in July 2005, the country is trying to recover from the long period of instability despite a still-fragile political situation.

Beginning around 2005, drug traffickers based in Latin America began to use Guinea-Bissau, along with several neighboring West African nations, as a transshipment point to Europe for

Bula, Guinea-Bissau

cocaine. The nation was described by a United Nations official as being at risk for becoming a "narco-state". The government and the military have done little to stop drug trafficking, which has increased since the 2012 coup d'état.

Guinea-Bissau is a member of the Organization for the Harmonization of Business Law in Africa (OHADA).

Demographics

Ethnic groups

Crossing the river at low tide

The population of Guinea-Bissau is ethnically diverse and has many distinct languages, customs, and social structures. Guinea-Bissauans can be divided into the following ethnic groups: Fula and the Mandinka-speaking people, who comprise the largest portion of the population and are concentrated in the north and northeast; the Balanta and Papel people, who live in the southern coastal regions; and the Manjaco and Mancanha, who occupy the central and northern coastal areas. Most of the remainder are *mestiços* of mixed Portuguese and African descent, including a Cape Verdean minority.

Portuguese natives comprise a very

small percentage of Guinea-Bissauans. This deficit was directly caused by the exodus of Portuguese settlers that took place after Guinea-Bissau gained independence. The country has a tiny Chinese population, including those of mixed Portuguese and Chinese ancestry from Macau, a former Asian Portuguese colony.

Language

Only 14% of the population speaks the official language, Portuguese. 44% speak Kriol, a Portuguese-based creole language, and the remainder speaks native African languages. Most Portuguese and Mestiços speak one of the African languages and Kriol as second languages. French is learned in schools, as the country is surrounded by French-speaking countries and is a full member of the Francophonie.

Religion

Religion in Guinea-Bissau

religion	percent
Islam	50%
Indigenous	40%
Christianity	10%

Throughout the 20th century, most Bissau-Guineans practiced some form of Animism. Recently, many have adopted Islam, which is currently practiced by 50% of the country's population; most of Guinea-Bissau's Muslims practice Sunni Islam. Approximately 10 percent of the country's population belong to the Christian community, and 40% continue to hold Indigenous beliefs. These statistics can be misleading, however, as both Islamic and Christian practices may be largely influenced and enriched by syncretism with traditional African beliefs.

Health

The WHO estimates that there are fewer than 5 physicians per 100,000 persons in the country, down from 12 per 100,000 in 2007. The prevalence of HIV-infection among the adult population is 1.8%, with only 20% of infected pregnant women receiving anti retroviral coverage. Malaria is an even bigger killer; 9% of the population have reported infection, and it is the specific mortality cause almost three times as often as AIDS. (In 2008, fewer than half of children younger than five slept under antimalaria nets or had access to antimalarial drugs).

Life expectancy at birth has climbed since 1990, but remains short: the WHO's estimate of life expectancy for a child born in 2008 was 49 years (and only 47 years for a boy).

Despite lowering rates in surrounding countries, cholera rates were reported in November 2012 to be on the rise, with 1,500 cases reported and nine deaths. A 2008 cholera epidemic in Guinea-Bissau affected 14,222 people and killed 225.

Maternal and child healthcare

In June 2011, the United Nations Population Fund released a report on The State of the World's Midwifery. It contained new data on the midwifery workforce and policies relating to newborn and maternal mortality for 58 countries. The 2010 maternal mortality rate per 100,000 births for Guinea Bissau is 1000. This is compared with 804.3 in 2008 and 966 in 1990. The under 5 mortality rate, per 1,000 births is 195 and the neonatal mortality as a percentage of under 5's mortality is 24. The aim of this report is to highlight ways in which the Millennium Development Goals can be achieved, particularly Goal 4 – Reduce child mortality and Goal 5 – improve maternal death. In Guinea Bissau the number of midwives per 1,000 live births is 3; one out of eighteen pregnant women die as a result of pregnancy.

Education

Education is compulsory from the age of 7 to 13. The enrollment of boys is higher than that of girls. Child labor is very common. A significant minority of the population are illiterate.

On the other side, Guinea-Bissau has several secondary schools (general as well as technical) and a surprising number of universities, to which an institutionally autonomous Faculty of Law as well as a Faculty of Medicine have to be added.

In 1998, the gross primary enrollment rate was 53.5 percent, with higher enrollment ratio for males (67.7 percent) compared to females (40 percent). Since 2001, Guinea-Bissau has been recovering from the civil conflict of 1999, and later conflicts, which displaced one-third of the population, destroyed many schools, and prevented most young children from attending school for at least half a year.

Culture

Carnival in Bissau

Music

The music of Guinea-Bissau is usually associated with the polyrhythmic gumbe genre, the country's primary musical export. However, civil unrest and other factors have combined over the years to keep gumbe, and other genres, out of mainstream audiences, even in generally syncretist African countries.

The calabash is the primary musical instrument of Guinea-Bissau, and is used in extremely swift and rhythmically complex dance music. Lyrics are almost always in Guinea-Bissau Creole, a Portuguese-based creole language, and are often humorous and topical, revolving around current events and controversies, especially AIDS.

The word *gumbe* is sometimes used generically, to refer to any music of the country, although it most specifically refers to a unique style that fuses about ten of the country's folk music traditions. Tina and tinga are other popular genres, while extent folk traditions include ceremonial music used in funerals, initiations and other rituals, as well as Balanta brosca and kussundé, Mandinga djambadon, and the kundere sound of the Bissagos Islands.

Film

Flora Gomes is an internationally renowned film director; his most famous film is "Nha Fala", English: "My Voice". Gomes' *Mortu Nega* (Death Denied) (1988) was the first fiction film and the second feature film ever made in Guinea-Bissau. (The first feature film was N'tturudu, by director Umban u'Kest in 1987.) At FESPACO 1989, Mortu Nega won the prestigious Oumarou Ganda Prize. Mortu Nega is in Creole language with English subtitles. In 1992, Gomes directed Udju Azul di Yonta, which was screened in the Un Certain Regard section at the 1992 Cannes Film Festival. Gomes has also served on the boards of many Africa-centric film festivals.

Source http://en.wikipedia.org/wiki/Guinea-Bissau

History of Guinea-Bissau

The **history of Guinea-Bissau** was dominated by Portugal from the 1450s to the 1970s; since independence, the country has been primarily controlled by a single-party system.

Portuguese Rule

Coats of arms of Portuguese Guinea-Bissau

The rivers of Guinea and the islands of Cape Verde were among the first areas in Africa explored by the Portuguese. Portugal claimed Portuguese Guinea in 1446, but few trading posts were established before 1600. With the cooperation of some local tribes, the Portuguese entered the slave trade and exported large numbers of Africans to the Western Hemisphere via the Cape Verde Islands. Cacheu became one of the major slave centers, and a small fort still stands in the town. The local African rulers in Guinea, who prospered greatly from the African slave trade, had no interest in allowing the Europeans any further inland than the fortified coastal settlements where the trading takes place. The slave trade declined in the 19th century, the major commercial center. Portuguese conquest and consolidation of the interior did not begin until the latter half of the 19th century. Portugal lost part of Guinea to French West Africa, including the center of earlier Portuguese commercial interest, the Casamance River region. A dispute with Britain over the island of Bolama was settled in Portugal's favor with the involvement of U.S. President Ulysses S. Grant. The interior of Portuguese Guinea was brought under control after more than 30 years of fighting. The administrative capital was moved from Bolama to Bissau in 1941, and in 1952, by constitutional amendment, the colony of Portuguese Guinea became an overseas province of Portugal.

Struggle for independence

Amílcar Cabral, with the flag of Guinea-Bissau on a stamp

In 1956, the African Party for the Independence of Guinea and Cape Verde (PAIGC) was organized clandestinely

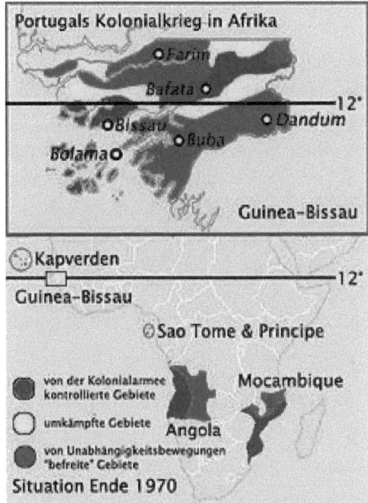

Portuguese-held (green), disputed (yellow) and rebel-held areas (red) in Portuguese-Guinea and other colonies 1970

by Amílcar Cabral and Rafael Barbosa. The PAIGC moved its headquarters to Conakry, Guinea, in 1960 and started an armed rebellion against the Portuguese in 1961 (for a detailed account of this struggle, see the PAIGC page). Despite the presence of Portuguese troops, which grew to more than 35,000, the PAIGC steadily expanded its influence until, by 1968, it controlled most of the country. It established civilian rule in the territory under its control and held elections for a National Assembly. Portuguese forces and civilians increasingly were confined to their garrisons and larger towns. The Portuguese Governor and Commander in Chief from 1968 to 1973, General António de Spínola, returned to Portugal and led the movement which brought democracy to Portugal and independence for its colonies.

On 6 February 1969, the Cheche Disaster saw the death of almost fifty Portuguese soldiers while crossing the Corubal River.

Amílcar Cabral was assassinated in Conakry in 1973, and party leadership fell to Aristides Pereira, who later became the first president of the Republic of Cape Verde. The PAIGC National Assembly met at Boe in the southeastern region and declared the independence of Guinea-Bissau on 24 September 1973 and was recognized by a 93-7 UN General Assembly vote in November, unprecedented as it denounced illegal Portuguese aggression and occupation and was prior to complete control and Portuguese recognition. Following Portugal's April 1974 Carnation Revolution, it granted independence to Guinea-Bissau on 10 September 1974. Luís Cabral, Amílcar Cabral's half-brother, became President of Guinea-Bissau.

Independence from Portugal

Following Portugal's April 1974 Carnation Revolution, it granted independence to Guinea-Bissau on 10 September 1974. Luís Cabral, Amílcar Cabral's half-brother, became President of Guinea-Bissau. Following independence local soldiers that fought along with the Portuguese Army against the PAIGC guerrillas were slaughtered by the thousands. A small number escaped to Portugal or to other African nations. The most famous massacre occurred in Bissorã. In 1980 PAIGC admitted in its newspaper "Nó Pintcha" (dated 29 November 1980) that many were executed and buried in unmarked collective graves in the woods of Cumerá, Portogole and Mansabá. In late 1980, the government was overthrown in a relatively bloodless coup led by Prime Minister and former armed forces commander João Bernardo Vieira.

Vieira's presidency

From November 1980 to May 1984, power was held by a provisional government responsible to a Revolutionary Council headed by President João Bernardo Vieira. In 1984, the council was dissolved, and the National Popular Assembly (ANP) was reconstituted. The single-party assembly approved a new constitution, elected President Vieira to a new 5-year term, and elected a Council of State, which was the executive agent of the ANP. Under this system, the president presides over the Council of State and serves as head of state and government. The president also was head of the PAIGC and commander in chief of the armed forces.

From 1980 to 1991, opposition parties were illegal. Aristide Menezes led the Democratic Front, which in 1991 became the first legal opposition party and paved the way for democratic elections.

Democracy

In 1994, 20 years after independence from Portugal, the country's first multiparty legislative and presidential elections were held. An army uprising that triggered the Guinea-Bissau Civil War in 1998, created hundreds of thousands of displaced persons. The president was ousted by a military junta in 7 May 1999. An interim government turned over power in February 2000 when opposition leader Kumba Ialá took office following two rounds of transparent presidential elections. Guinea-Bissau's transition back to democracy has been complicated by a crippled economy devastated by civil war and the military's predilection for governmental meddling.

In September 2003 a bloodless coup took place in which the military, headed by General Veríssimo Correia Seabra, arrested Ialá, because "he was unable to solve the problems". After being delayed several times, legislative elections were held in April 2004.

A mutiny of military factions in October 2004 resulted in the death of General Seabra and others, and caused widespread unrest. The Prime Minister Carlos Gomes Júnior has stated that the mutineers were ex-United Nations soldiers recently returned from Liberia who were angry about delays in being paid. Talks between these soldiers and the authorities have so far failed to come to an agreement.

In June 2005, presidential elections were held for the first time since the coup that deposed Ialá. Ialá returned as the candidate for the PRS, claiming to be the legitimate president of the country, but the election was won by former president João Bernardo Vieira, deposed in the 1998 coup. Vieira was a candidate for one sect of the PAIGC. Vieira defeated Malam Bacai Sanha in a runoff-election, but Sanha refused initially to concede, claiming that the elections had been fraudulent in two constituencies, including the capital Bissau.

Despite reports that there had been an influx of arms in the weeks leading up to the election and reports of some 'disturbances during campaigning' - including attacks on the presidential palace and the Interior Ministry by as-yet-unidentified gunmen - European monitors labelled the election as "calm and organized".

Source http://en.wikipedia.org/wiki/History_of_Guinea-Bissau

Jeta (Guinea-Bissau)

Jeta is an island in the Bissagos Islands, Guinea-Bissau. Its area is 109 km².

Source http://en.wikipedia.org/wiki/Jeta_(Guinea-Bissau)

João Viera

João Viera is an important sea turtle nesting island in the Bijagós Archipelago of Guinea-Bissau. It is also a centre for sea fishing and is the centre of the João Viera Marine Park.

Source: http://en.wikipedia.org/wiki/João_Viera

List of heads of government of Guinea-Bissau

Prime Minister of the Republic of Guinea-Bissau

Emblem of Guinea-Bissau

Incumbent

Rui Duarte de Barros

Acting

since 16 May 2012

Appointer	Manuel Serifo Nhamadjo, as Acting President
Inaugural holder	Francisco Mendes
Formation	24 September 1973

Prime Ministers of Guinea-Bissau (1973–Present)

(Dates in italics indicate *de facto* continuation of office)

Tenure	Portrait	Incumbent
State of Guinea-Bissau	*Unilateral Declaration of Independence*	
24 September 1973 to 10 September 1974		Francisco Mendes, Prime Minister
State of Guinea-Bissau	*Independence recognized by Portugal*	
10 September 1974 to 13 March 1977		Francisco Mendes, Prime Minister
Republic of Guinea-Bissau *(República da Guiné-Bissau)*		
13 March 1977 to 7 July 1978		Francisco Mendes, Prime Minister
7 July 1978 to 28 September 1978		Constantino Teixeira, Prime Minister
28 September 1978 to 14 November 1980		João Bernardo Vieira, Prime Minister
14 November 1980 to 14 May 1982	*Vacant*	
14 May 1982 to 10 March 1984		Victor Saúde Maria, Prime Minister
10 March 1984 to 27 December 1991	*Post abolished*	
27 December 1991 to 26 October 1994		Carlos Correia, Prime Minister
26		Manuel Saturnino

Tenure	Portrait	Incumbent
October 1994 to 6 June 1997		da Costa, Prime Minister
6 June 1997 to 3 December 1998		Carlos Correia, Prime Minister
3 December 1998 to 19 February 2000		Francisco Fadul, Prime Minister
19 February 2000 to 19 March 2001		Caetano N'Tchama, Prime Minister
21 March 2001 to 9 December 2001		Faustino Imbali, Prime Minister
9 December 2001 to 17 November 2002		Alamara Nhassé, Prime Minister
17 November 2002 to 14 September 2003		Mário Pires, Prime Minister
14 September 2003 to 28 September 2003		Vacant
28 September 2003 to 10 May 2004		Artur Sanhá, Prime Minister
10 May 2004 to 2 November 2005		Carlos Gomes Júnior, Prime Minister
2 November 2005 to 13 April 2007		Aristides Gomes, Prime Minister
13 April 2007 to 5 August 2008		Martinho Ndafa Kabi, Prime Minister
5 August 2008 to 2 January 2009		Carlos Correia, Prime Minister
2 January 2009 to 10 February 2012		Carlos Gomes Júnior, Prime Minister
10 February 2012 to 12 April 2012		Adiato Djaló Nandigna, Acting Prime Minister
12 April 2012 to 16 May 2012		Vacant
16 May 2012 to 9 Present		Rui Duarte de Barros, Acting Prime Minister

Affiliations

PAIGC Partido Africano da Independência de Guiné e Cabo Verde
(African Party for the Independence of Guinea and Cape Verde) *marxist, only legal party 1974-1991, to 1980 pro-union with Cape Verde*

PRS Partido para a Renovaçao Social
(Party for Social Renewal) *progressive*

Mil Military

n-p non-partisan

Source http://en.wikipedia.org/wiki/List_of_heads_of_government_of_Guinea-Bissau

List of heads of state of Guinea-Bissau

President of the

Republic of Guinea-Bissau

Emblem of Guinea-Bissau

Incumbent

Manuel Serifo Nhamadjo

Acting

since 11 May 2012
Term length 5 years
Inaugural holder Luís Cabral
Formation 24 September 1973

Presidents of Guinea-Bissau (1973–Present)

(Dates in italics indicate *de facto* continuation of office)

Tenure	Portrait	Incumbent
State of Guinea-Bissau		*Unilateral Declaration of Ind*

List of heads of state of Guinea-Bissau • 19

24 September 1973 to 10 September 1974		**Luís Cabral**, Chairman of the Council of State
State of Guinea-Bissau	*Independence recognized by P*	
10 September 1974 to 13 March 1977		**Luís Cabral**, Chairman of the Council of State
Republic of Guinea-Bissau *(República da Guiné-Bissau)*		
13 March 1977 to 14 November 1980		**Luís Cabral**, Chairman of the Council of State
14 November 1980 to 14 May 1984		**João Bernard Vieira**, Chairman of the Council of the Revolution
14 May 1984 to 16 May 1984		**Carmen Pereira**, Acting President
16 May 1984 to 29 September 1994		**João Bernard Vieira**, Chairman of the Council of State
29 September 1994 to 7 May 1999		**João Bernard Vieira**, President
7 May 1999 to 14 May 1999	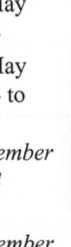	**Ansumane Mané**, Chairman of the Supreme Command of the Military Junta
14 May 1999 to 17 February 2000	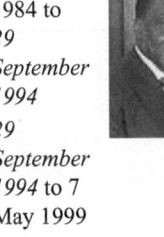	**Malam Bacai Sanhá**, Acting President
17 February 2000 to 14 September 2003		**Kumba Ialá**, President
14 September 2003 to 28 September 2003		**Veríssimo Correia Seabra**, Chairman of the Military Committee for the Restoration of Constitutional and Democratic Order
28 September 2003 to 1 October 2005		**Henrique Rosa**, Acting President
1 October 2005 to 2 March 2009		**João Bernard Vieira**, President
3 March 2009 to 8 September 2009		**Raimundo Pereira**, Acting President
8 September 2009 to 9 January 2012	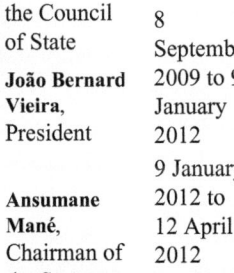	**Malam Bacai Sanhá**, President
9 January 2012 to 12 April 2012		**Raimundo Pereira**, Acting President
12 April 2012 to		**Mamadu Tur Kuruma**, Chairman of the Military Command
11 May 2012 to Present		**Manuel Serifo Nhamadjo**, Acting President

Affiliations

PAIGC	**Partido Africano da Independência de Guiné e Cabo Verde** (African Party for the Independence of Guinea and Cape Verde) *marxist, only legal party 1974-1991, to 1980 pro-union with Cape Verde*
PRS	**Partido para a Renovação Social** (Party for Social Renewal) *progressive*
Mil	Military
n-p	non-partisan

Latest election

Guinea-Bissau presidential election, 20

Party	Candidate	First round Votes	Per
African Party for the Independence of Guinea and Cape Verde	Carlos Gomes Júnior	154,797	48.9
Party for Social Renewal	Mohamed Ialá Embaló	73,842	23.3
Independent	Manuel Serifo Nhamadjo	49,767	15.7
Independent	Henrique Pereira Rosa	17,070	5.40
Independent	Baciro Djá	10,298	3.26
Democratic Alliance	Vicente Fernandes	4,396	1.39
Workers' Party	Aregado Mantenque Té	3,300	1.04
Guinean Salvation Democratic Socialist	Serifo Baldé	1,463	0.46

Party – Young Party				Total (turnout 55%/...)	316,107	100
Independent	Luís Nancassa	1,174	0.3?			

Source: African Elections Database
Source http://en.wikipedia.org/wiki/List_of_heads_of_state_of_Guinea-Bissau

Orango

Orango is one of the Bijagós Islands, located 60 kilometers (38 miles) off the coast of mainland Guinea-Bissau. It is the centre of the Ilhas de Orango National Park and has one town, Eticoga.

Orango is known for its saltwater hippopotamuses.

Matrimonial traditions

Orango's inhabitants developed a number of distinct matrimonial traditions which are unique with respect to the role played by women. Marriage is formally proposed by women — their choice of spouse is made public to the groom-to-be and the rest of the community by an offer of a dish of specially prepared fish, marinated in red palm oil. According to tradition, the offer is accepted by eating the fish, and cannot be turned down without dishonor. The marriage becomes official months later, after the bride-to-be, with no help from the groom, builds the couple a new home out of driftwood, blond grass, and mud bricks.

In recent years the island's traditions are competing with outside influences, both economic and religious. Men increasingly travel to the mainland to work, bringing back the mainland's trappings and ideas. Men and women have adopted religious practices introduced by Protestant missionaries, which have also reduced the influences of the island's matrimonial traditions.

Source http://en.wikipedia.org/wiki/Orango

Orangozinho

Orangozinho is an island in the Bissagos Islands, Guinea-Bissau. Its area is 107 km².

Source http://en.wikipedia.org/wiki/Orangozinho

Outline of Guinea-Bissau

The Flag of Guinea-Bissau

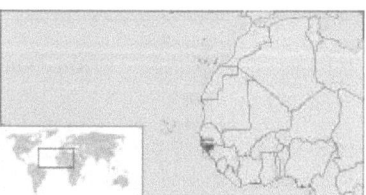

The location of Guinea-Bissau

The **Republic of Guinea-Bissau** is a sovereign country located in West Africa. Guinea-Bissau is the 8th least extensive country in continental Africa.

An enlargeable map of the Republic of Guinea-Bissau

It is bordered by Senegal to the north, and Guinea to the south and east, with the Atlantic Ocean to its west. Formerly the Portuguese colony of Portuguese Guinea, upon independence, the name of its capital, Bissau, was added to the country's name in order to prevent confusion between itself and the Republic of Guinea.

The following outline is provided as an overview of and topical guide to Guinea-Bissau:

General reference

An enlargeable relief map of Guinea-Bissau

Pronunciation: /ˌɡɪni bɨˈsaʊ/
Common English country name: Guinea-Bissau
Official English country name: The Re-

public of Guinea-Bissau
Common endonym(s):
Official endonym(s):
Adjectival(s): Guinean
Demonym(s):
Etymology: Name of Guinea-Bissau
ISO country codes: GW, GNB, 624
ISO region codes: See ISO 3166-2:GW
Internet country code top-level domain: .gw

Geography of Guinea-Bissau

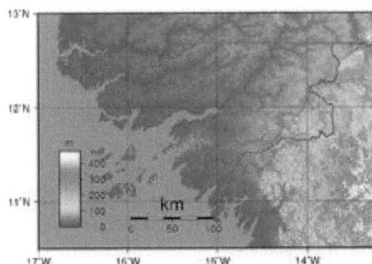

An enlargeable topographic map of Guinea-Bissau

Guinea-Bissau is: a country
Population of Guinea-Bissau: 1,695,000 - 147th most populous country
Area of Guinea-Bissau: 36544 km
Atlas of Guinea-Bissau

Location
Guinea-Bissau is situated within the following regions:
Northern Hemisphere and Western Hemisphere
Africa
West Africa
Time zone: Coordinated Universal Time UTC+00
Extreme points of Guinea-Bissau
High: unnamed location in the northeast corner of the country 310 m (1,017 ft)
Low: North Atlantic Ocean 0 m
Land boundaries: 724 km
▮ Guinea 386 km
▮ Senegal 338 km
Coastline: North Atlantic Ocean 350 km

Environment of Guinea-Bissau
Climate of Guinea-Bissau
Environmental issues in Guinea-Bissau
Ecoregions in Guinea-Bissau
Renewable energy in Guinea-Bissau

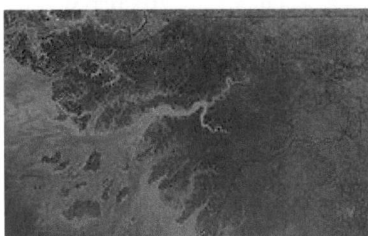

An enlargeable satellite image of Guinea-Bissau

Geology of Guinea-Bissau
Protected areas of Guinea-Bissau
Biosphere reserves in Guinea-Bissau
National parks of Guinea-Bissau
Wildlife of Guinea-Bissau
Flora of Guinea-Bissau
Fauna of Guinea-Bissau
Birds of Guinea-Bissau
Mammals of Guinea-Bissau

Natural geographic features of Guinea-Bissau
Glaciers in Guinea-Bissau: none
Islands of Guinea-Bissau
Lakes of Guinea-Bissau
Mountains of Guinea-Bissau
Volcanoes in Guinea-Bissau
Rivers of Guinea-Bissau
Waterfalls of Guinea-Bissau
Valleys of Guinea-Bissau
World Heritage Sites in Guinea-Bissau: None

Regions of Guinea-Bissau

Ecoregions of Guinea-Bissau
Main article: Ecoregions in Guinea-Bissau

Administrative divisions of Guinea-Bissau
Main article: Administrative divisions of Guinea-Bissau
Regions of Guinea-Bissau
Sectors of Guinea-Bissau

Regions of Guinea-Bissau

Sectors of Guinea-Bissau

Municipalities of Guinea-Bissau
Capital of Guinea-Bissau: Bissau
Cities of Guinea-Bissau

Demography of Guinea-Bissau
Main article: Demographics of Guinea-Bissau

Government and politics of Guinea-Bissau
Main article: Government of Guinea-Bissau and Politics of Guinea-Bissau
Form of government: semi-presidential representative democratic republic
Capital of Guinea-Bissau: Bissau
Elections in Guinea-Bissau
Political parties in Guinea-Bissau
Political scandals of Guinea-Bissau
Taxation in Guinea-Bissau

Branches of the government of Guinea-Bissau

Executive branch of the government of Guinea-Bissau
Head of state: President of Guinea-Bissau, Malam Bacai Sanhá
Head of government: Prime Minister of Guinea-Bissau, Carlos Gomes Júnior
Cabinet of Guinea-Bissau

Legislative branch of the government of Guinea-Bissau
Parliament of Guinea-Bissau (unicameral)

Judicial branch of the government of Guinea-Bissau
Supreme Court of Guinea-Bissau

Foreign relations of Guinea-Bissau
Diplomatic missions in Guinea-Bissau
Diplomatic missions of Guinea-Bissau

International organization membership
The Republic of Guinea-Bissau is a member of:
African, Caribbean, and Pacific Group of States (ACP)
African Development Bank Group (AfDB)
African Union (AU)
Comunidade dos Países de Língua Portuguesa (CPLP)
Conference des Ministres des Finances des Pays de la Zone Franc (FZ)
International Telecommunicati Satellite Organization (IT! International Trac Union Confederation (ITUC)
Islamic Development Bar (IDB)
Multilateral Investment Guarantee Agenc (MIGA)

Economic Community of West African States (ECOWAS)
Food and Agriculture Organization (FAO)
Group of 77 (G77)
International Bank for Reconstruction and Development (IBRD)
International Civil Aviation Organization (ICAO)
International Criminal Court (ICCt) (signatory)
International Criminal Police Organization (Interpol)
International Development Association (IDA)
International Federation of Red Cross and Red Crescent Societies (IFRCS)
International Finance Corporation (IFC)
International Fund for Agricultural Development (IFAD)
International Labour Organization (ILO)
International Maritime Organization (IMO)
International Monetary Fund (IMF)
International Olympic Committee (IOC)
International Organization for Migration (IOM)
International Red Cross and Red Crescent Movement (ICRM)
International Telecommunication Union (ITU)
Nonaligned Movement (NAM)
Organisation internationale de Francophonie (O
Organisation of Islamic Cooperation (OIC)
Organization for Prohibition of Chemical Weapons (OPCW)
União Latina
United Nations (U
United Nations Conference on Trade and Development (UNCTAD)
United Nations Educational, Scientific, and Cultural Organization (UNESCO)
United Nations Industrial Development Organization (UNIDO)
Universal Postal Union (UPU)
West African Development Bank (WADB) (regional)
West African Economic and Monetary Union (WAEMU)
World Federation of Trade Unions (WFTU)
World Health Organization (WHO)
World Intellectual Property Organization (WIPO)
World Meteorological Organization (WMO)
World Tourism Organization (UNWTO)
World Trade Organization (WTO)

Law and order in Guinea-Bissau

Main article: Law of Guinea-Bissau
Constitution of Guinea-Bissau
Crime in Guinea-Bissau
Human rights in Guinea-Bissau
LGBT rights in Guinea-Bissau
Freedom of religion in Guinea-Bissau
Law enforcement in Guinea-Bissau

Military of Guinea-Bissau

Main article: Military of Guinea-Bissau
Command
Commander-in-chief:
Ministry of Defence of Guinea-Bissau
Forces
Army of Guinea-Bissau
Navy of Guinea-Bissau
Air Force of Guinea-Bissau
Special forces of Guinea-Bissau
Military history of Guinea-Bissau
Military ranks of Guinea-Bissau

Local government in Guinea-Bissau

History of Guinea-Bissau

Main article: History of Guinea-Bissau, Timeline of the history of Guinea-Bissau, and Current events of Guinea-Bissau
Military history of Guinea-Bissau

Culture of Guinea-Bissau

Main article: Culture of Guinea-Bissau
Architecture of Guinea-Bissau
Cuisine of Guinea-Bissau
Festivals in Guinea-Bissau
Languages of Guinea-Bissau
Media in Guinea-Bissau
National symbols of Guinea-Bissau
Coat of arms of Guinea-Bissau
Flag of Guinea-Bissau
National anthem of Guinea-Bissau
People of Guinea-Bissau
Prostitution in Guinea-Bissau
Public holidays in Guinea-Bissau
Records of Guinea-Bissau
Religion in Guinea-Bissau
Christianity in Guinea-Bissau
Hinduism in Guinea-Bissau
Islam in Guinea-Bissau
Judaism in Guinea-Bissau
Sikhism in Guinea-Bissau
World Heritage Sites in Guinea-Bissau: None

Art in Guinea-Bissau

Art in Guinea-Bissau
Cinema of Guinea-Bissau
Literature of Guinea-Bissau
Music of Guinea-Bissau
Television in Guinea-Bissau
Theatre in Guinea-Bissau

Sports in Guinea-Bissau

Main article: Sports in Guinea-Bissau
Football in Guinea-Bissau
Guinea-Bissau at the Olympics

Economy and infrastructure of Guinea-Bissau

Main article: Economy of Guinea-Bissau
Economic rank, by nominal GDP (2007): 182nd (one hundred and eighty second)
Agriculture in Guinea-Bissau
Banking in Guinea-Bissau
National Bank of Guinea-Bissau
Communications in Guinea-Bissau
Internet in Guinea-Bissau
Companies of Guinea-Bissau
Currency of Guinea-Bissau: Franc
ISO 4217: XOF
Energy in Guinea-Bissau
Energy policy of Guinea-Bissau
Oil industry in Guinea-Bissau
Health care in Guinea-Bissau
Mining in Guinea-Bissau
Guinea-Bissau Stock Exchange
Tourism in Guinea-Bissau
Transport in Guinea-Bissau
Airports in Guinea-Bissau
Rail transport in Guinea-Bissau
Roads in Guinea-Bissau

Education in Guinea-Bissau

Main article: Education in Guinea-Bissau
Source http://en.wikipedia.org/wiki/Outline_of_Guinea-Bissau

Pecixe

Pecixe is an island or group of islands in the Bissagos Islands, Guinea-Bissau. The area is 168 km². The language of the island or islands is reported to be Mandjak, a language of Guinea-Bissau with over 72,000 speakers altogether.

Navigation menu

Personal tools
Create account
Log in

Namespaces
Article
Talk

Variants

Actions

Search

Navigation
Main page
Contents
Featured content
Current events
Random article
Donate to Wikipedia

Interaction
Help
About Wikipedia
Community portal
Recent changes
Contact Wikipedia

Toolbox
What links here
Related changes
Upload file

Special pages
Permanent link
Page information
Cite this page

Print/export
Create a book
Download as PDF
Printable version

Languages
Deutsch
Español
Edit links
Source   http://en.wikipedia.org/wiki/Pecixe

Politics of Guinea-Bissau

takes place in a framework of a semi-presidential representative democratic republic in transition, whereby the President is head of state and the Prime Minister is head of government, and of a multi-party system. Executive power is exercised by the government. Legislative power is vested in both the government and the National People's Assembly. Since 1994 the party system is dominated by the socialist African Independence Party of Guinea and Cape Verde and the Party for Social Renewal. The Judiciary is independent of the executive and the legislature.

Despite the democratic, constitutional framework, the military has exercised substantial power and interfered repeatedly in civilian leadership since multi-party elections were instituted in 1994. In the past 16 years, Guinea Bissau has experienced two coups, a civil war, an attempted coup, and a presidential assassination by the military. No president has served a full 5-year term.

Political developments

In Guinea-Bissau in 1989, the ruling African Independence Party of Guinea

President palace in Guinea-Bissau

and Cape Verde (PAIGC) under the direction of President João Bernardo "Nino" Vieira began to outline a political liberalization program which the People's National Assembly approved in 1991. Reforms that paved the way for multi-party democracy included the repeal of articles of the constitution, which had enshrined the leading role of the PAIGC. Laws were ratified to allow the formation of other political parties, a free press, and independent trade unions with the right to strike.

Guinea-Bissau's first multi-party elections for president and parliament were held in 1994. Following the 1998-99 civil war, presidential and legislative elections were again held, bringing opposition leader Kumba Ialá and his Party for Social Renewal to power. Ialá was ousted in a bloodless coup in September 2003 and Henrique Rosa was sworn in as President.

Former President Viera was once again elected as President in July 2005. The government of Prime Minister Carlos Gomes Júnior was elected in March 2004 in a free and fair election round, but was replaced by the government of Prime Minister Aristides Gomes which took office already in November 2005. Aristides Gomes lost a no-confidence vote and submitted his resignation in March 2007. Martinho Ndafa Kabi was proposed as prime minister by a coalition composed of the PAIGC, the Social Renewal Party (PRS), and the United Social Democratic Party (PUSD). On April 9, it was announced that President João Bernardo Vieira had rejected the choice of Kabi, but the coalition said that they maintained him as their choice and later on the same day, Vieira appointed Kabi as the new prime minister. He took office on April 13, and his government, composed of 20 ministers (including eight from the PAIGC, eight from the PRS, and two from the PUSD) was named on April 17.

2009 assassination

President Viera was reported killed on March 2, 2009 by soldiers as retaliation for the killing of the head of the joint chiefs of staff, General Tagme Na Waie, who was killed the previous day.

2010 military unrest

Prior to the 2008 election, a decision to change the electoral date and extend the parliamentary mandate resulted in major controversy when the Assembly deputies snubbed the president and chose to extend their mandate. After the Supreme Court annulled that law, President Vieira dissolved the Assembly, thus allowing the standing committee to continue working, and appointed a new government composed of loyalists.

Rear Admiral Bubo Na Tchuto tried to organize a coup on August 7, 2008, but was pre-empted and arrested; however, he managed to escape the country. The attempted coup added to instability ahead of parliamentary elections. Gambia subsequently arrested Bubo Na Tchuto. He later returned to Guinea-Bissau disguised as a fisherman and took refuge at a UN compound. Although the UN agreed to surrender him to the government, he continued to reside in the compound. As a result of his return security in the country was tightened, contributing to uncertainty and instability.

On April 1, 2010, soldiers entered UN offices and left with Bubo Na Tchuto. The same day, soldiers entered Prime Minister Carlos Gomes Júnior's residence and held him on the premises. Simultaneously, forty military officers, including Zamora Induta, head of Guinea-Bissau's armed forces, were being held at an army base. Hundreds of the PM's supporters demanded his release. In response, the deputy army chief, Antonio Ndjai, said: "If the people continue to go out into the streets to show their support for Carlos Gomes Junior, then I will kill Carlos Gomes Junior ... or I will send someone to kill him." The following day the PM was taken to meet with the president where he said: "I will not resign because I was democratically elected. I consider what happened on Thursday as an incident. The situation is now stable. I can assure you that institutions will return to their normal functions." The UN secretary general and other international powers condemned the move, while government ministers issued a statement saying "Members of government expressed their support and their attachment to the prime minister and firmly condemned the use of force as a means to resolve problems." Tensions seemingly calmed with President Sanha saying the coup attempt was "a confusion between soldiers that reached the government;" and the UN Secretary General spoke about the PM's "detention and subsequent release." Nevertheless while the members of the cabinet and the international community condemned the attempted coup and talked about the PM's release, reports still indicated that "renegade soldiers" had the PM "under guard."

2011 attempted coup

After Army chief of staff General Antonio Indjai was reported to have been arrested under the orders of navy chief Rear Admiral Jose Americo Bubo Na Tchuto, his troops freed him while Prime Minister Carlos Gomes Júnior went to seek asylum at the Angolan embassy. Indjai then said that his naval counterpart had been arrested. The events occurred while President Malam Bacai Sanha had been in Paris, France for medical care.

2012 coup

On 12 April 2012 the military took over the central district of the capital. As of Thursday the whereabouts of the country's interim president and prime minister are unknown. On 16 April, military leaders and a coalition\ of political parties announced the formation of a Transitional National Council, under international pressure.

Executive branch

Office	Name	Party	Sin
Acting President	Manuel Serifo Nhamadjo	Independent	11 Ma 201
Acting Prime Minister	Rui Duarte de Barros	Independent	16 Ma 201

The president is elected by popular vote for a five-year term. The prime minister is appointed by the president after consultation with party leaders in the legislature.

Legislative branch

National People's Assembly.

The National People's Assembly (*Assembleia Nacional Popular*) has 102 members, elected for a four-year term in multi-member constituencies.

Political parties and elections

Candidates - Nominating parties	Votes 1st round	% 1st round	Votes 2nd round	% 2 r
Malam Bacai Sanhá - African Independence Party of Guinea and Cape Verde	158,276	35.45%	196,759	4 6
João Bernardo "Nino" Vieira - Independent	128,918	28.87%	216,167	5 3
Mohamed Ialá Embaló - Party for Social Renewal	111,606	25.00%	-	-
Francisco Fadul - United Social Democratic	12,733	2.85%	-	-

Parties	Votes	%	Seats
Party Aregado Mantenque Té - Workers' Party	9,000	2.02%	-
Mamadú Iaia Djaló - Independent	7,112	1.59%	-
Mário Lopes da Rosa - Independent	4,863	1.09%	-
Idrissa Djaló - National Unity Party	3,604	0.81%	-
Adelino Mano Queta - Independent	2,816	0.63%	-
Faustino Fadut Imbali - Manifest Party of the People	2,330	0.52%	-
Paulino Empossa Ié - Independent	2,215	0.50%	-
Antonieta Rosa Gomes - Guinean Civic Forum-Social Democracy	1,642	0.37%	-
João Tátis Sá - Guinean People's Party	1,378	0.31%	-
Total (turnout 87.6% / 78.6%)	**446,493**		**412,926**

Parties	Votes	%	Seats
African Independence Party of Guinea and Cape Verde (*Partido Africano da Independência de Guiné e Cabo Verde*)	145,316	33.88	45
Party for Social Renewal (*Partido para a Renovação Social*)	113,656	26.50	35
United Social Democratic Party (*Partido Unido Social Democrático*)	75,485	17.60	17
United Platform (*Plataforma Unida*)	20,700	4.83	-
Electoral Union (*União Eleitoral*)	18,354	4.28	2
Democratic Socialist Party (*Partido Democrático Socialista*)	8,789	2.05	-
Union for Change (*União para a Mudança*)	8,621	2.01	-
Resistance of Guinea-Bissau-Bafatá Movement (*Resistência da Guiné-Bissau-Movimento Bafatá*)	7,918	1.85	-
National Unity Party (*Partido da Unidade Nacional*)	6,260	1.46	-
United People's Alliance (*Aliança Popular Unida*)	5,817	1.36	1
National Union for Democracy and Progress (*União Nacional para a Democracia e o Progresso*)	5,042	1.18	-
Guinean Civic Forum-Social Democracy (*Fórum Cívico Guineense-Social Democracia*)	4,209	0.98	-
Guinean Democratic Movement (*Movimento Democrático Guineense*)	4,202	0.98	-
Manifest Party of the People (*Partido do Manifesto do Povo*)	3,402	0.79	-
Socialist Party of Guinea-Bissau (*Partido Socialista da Guiné-Bissau*)	1,167	0.27	-
Total (turnout 76.2%)	**428,937**	100.00	**100**
Registered voters	603,639		
Total votes cast	460,254		
Invalid votes	31,317		

Source: African Elections Database

Judicial branch

The Supreme Court (*Supremo Tribunal da Justiça*), consists of nine justices who are appointed by the president and serve at his pleasure, final court of appeals in criminal and civil case. There are Regional Courts, one in each of nine regions, first court of appeals for sectoral court decisions, hear all felony cases and civil cases valued at over $1,000 and 24 Sectoral Courts, judges are not necessarily trained lawyers, hear civil cases under $1,000 and misdemeanor criminal cases.

Administrative divisions

Guinea-Bissau is divided in 9 regions (*regioes*, singular - *regiao*); Bafata, Biombo, Bissau, Bolama, Cacheu, Gabu, Oio, Quinara, Tombali.

note: Bolama may have been renamed Bolama/Bijagos

International organization participation

ACCT (associate), ACP, AfDB, ECA, ECOWAS, FAO, FZ, G-77, IBRD, ICAO, ICFTU, ICRM, IDA, IDB, IFAD, IFC, IFRCS, ILO, IMF, IMO, Intelsat, Interpol, IOC, IOM, ITU, NAM, OAU, OIC, OPCW, UN, UNCTAD, UNESCO, UNIDO, UPU, WADB (regional), WAEMU, WFTU, WHO, WIPO, WMO, WToO, WTrO

Source http://en.wikipedia.org/wiki/Politics_of_Guinea-Bissau

Roxa

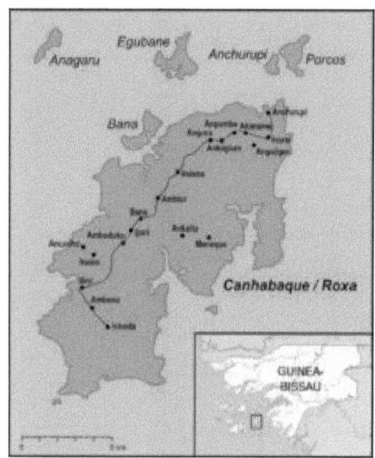

Island of Roxa/Canhabaque

Roxa (or **Canhabaque**) is an island in the Bissagos Islands, Guinea-Bissau. Its area is 111 km².

Navigation menu

Personal tools
Create account

Log in

Namespaces
Article
Talk

Variants

Actions

Search

Navigation
Main page
Contents
Featured content
Current events
Random article
Donate to Wikipedia

Interaction
Help
About Wikipedia
Community portal
Recent changes
Contact Wikipedia

Toolbox
What links here
Related changes
Upload file
Special pages
Permanent link
Page information
Cite this page

Print/export
Create a book
Download as PDF
Printable version

Languages
Deutsch
Español
Português
Română
中文
Edit links
Source   http://en.wikipedia.org/wiki/Roxa

Unhacomo

Unhacomo is an island in the Bissagos Islands of Guinea-Bissau.

Navigation menu

Personal tools
Create account
Log in

Namespaces
Article
Talk

Variants

Actions

Search

Navigation
Main page
Contents
Featured content
Current events
Random article
Donate to Wikipedia

Interaction
Help
About Wikipedia
Community portal
Recent changes
Contact Wikipedia

Toolbox
What links here
Related changes

Upload file
Special pages
Permanent link
Page information
Cite this page

Print/export
Create a book
Download as PDF
Printable version

Languages
Deutsch
Español
Edit links
Source   http://en.wikipedia.org/wiki/Unhacomo

Uno (Guinea-Bissau)

Uno is an island in the Bissagos Islands, Guinea-Bissau. Its area is 104 km.

Source   http://en.wikipedia.org/wiki/Uno_(Guinea-Bissau)

Uracane

Uracane is an island in the Bissagos Islands of Guinea-Bissau.

Navigation menu

Personal tools
Create account
Log in

Namespaces
Article
Talk

Variants

Actions

Search

Navigation
Main page
Contents
Featured content
Current events
Random article
Donate to Wikipedia

Interaction
Help
About Wikipedia
Community portal
Recent changes
Contact Wikipedia

Toolbox
What links here
Related changes

Upload file
Special pages
Permanent link
Page information
Cite this page

Print/export
Create a book
Download as PDF
Printable version

Languages
Edit links

Source http://en.wikipedia.org/wiki/Uracane